ABOUT T

David Mason, born 1960, studied Biology at Manchester University before embarking on a career in sales training with a large pharmaceutical company. From 1992 to 2000 he ran his own restaurant - Alfresco Eating House whilst working at schools and giving live poetry performances.

He is now a full-time writer and visits many schools to run Creative Writing and Poetry Workshops. Please contact him at the address overleaf if you would like him to appear at a school or venue near you.

"The Great Sweetshop Robbery and Other Poems" © David J. Mason 2001
Reprinted three times, this is the 4th edition.
Publishing address: North Street Publishing, 1 North Street,
North Walsham Norfolk NR28 9DH
Telephone 01692 406877

Cover Illustration © Nick Walmsley 2001
Contact address: Tryddyn, Horning Road West, Hoveton, Norfolk NR12 8QJ
Telephone 01603 782758

British Library Cataloguing-in-Publication Data
A Catalogue record for this book is available from the British Library
David J. Mason
ISBN 09521326 7 2

All rights reserved. No part of this book may be reproduced or utilised in any form or by any means, electronic or mechanical, including photocopying, recording, or by any information storage and retrieval system without permission in writing from the Publisher..

By the same author:
"Inside Out"   Poetry by David J. Mason published 1996
"Speaking Out"   Audio collection of selected work from "Inside Out" and "Get a Life"
"Get a Life"   Poetry collection published in 1997; illustrated by Nick Walmsley
"Seven Summers"   Poetry collection published in 1998
"Leo's Magic Shoes"   Children's novel published in 1999; illustrated by Kirsty Munro.
                        Reprinted as "Pedro's Magic Shoes" in 2000 with illustrations by
                        Nick Walmsley

Produced by Skippers Print & Copy Shop
53a The Green, Martham, Great Yarmouth, Norfolk NR29 4PF
Tel/Fax: 01493 740998 www.skippers-printers.co.uk

THE
POEMS

CREATION

On the first day God made kids.
On the second day God made furry bunnies, cuddly cats and fluffy dogs
For the children to play with.
On the third day He made chips
And on the fourth vanilla and later chocolate ice-cream.
God saw all this was good
And He wanted the kids to have more fun and
So invented swings and slides on the fifth day.
On the sixth day He made bunk beds and comfortable duvets
So that the kids could rest with Him on the seventh day.
On that day He was resting but set His alarm clock incorrectly.
On waking God became restless -
It was then He made His first and only mistake:
Teachers and parents.

BOYS V. GIRLS

Boys - If you ever think of weeing on an express train
Then take my advice and think again.
If you're a boy the story goes like this -
You're aiming as normal but then you miss.
You thought it was a bulls-eye
You thought it was the middle
But the target it moved
And you're covered in piddle.
You've yellow on your shoe
A damp patch on your pants
And if the others see you
They'll know it's not by chance.
You try to put the blower on
To dry things up a tad
But oops! You cannot keep your balance
Things are looking bad.
I'm afraid it's the end of the line for me
I'm never ever coming out
I just wish I was a girl instead
No aim to worry about.
You can sit upon your bottom
Feel the carriage sway
Concentrate upon it madly,
Let the wee go its own way.
So girls you mustn't complain
When you can't wee amongst the pines
You wouldn't want to be a boy
And pee on railway lines.

EAT UP YOUR VEG

An apple a day
Keeps the doctor away;
But I say
Try a sweetie
Or a biscuit
Or a lump of cake
Or a fizzy drink
Some chips
Or a chocolate milk shake.
A can of worms
A snail
A gorilla's armpit
A cup of snot
A pint of blood
Or a barrel load of sick -
But not a sprout
A carrot
Or a cauliflower cheese.
Take my advice -
Eat anything
But no more veggies
Please.

GERMS

Germs are in the beards
Of old men passing by
And on the tongues of raggedy cats
Too old to catch the mice.
Germs on my mate's yucky fingers
And in his sister's dirty hair,
Secret germs on toilet seats;
The germs are everywhere.
Living in the sewers
Which run beneath out street,
Stuck in bits of cheesy sock
They breed upon our feet.
Germs upon our handkerchiefs
And on our snotty fingers,
Germs that cannot be washed off
They fester there and linger.
Mum buys the things to kill germs,
Like Jif and Ajax cream,
But I don't know why she bothers
'Cos the germs just come back again
And again from kids with colds,
With sick and diarrhoea,
Warts, nose bleeds and eye ache -
Germs from too much beer.
So let me in conclusion
Tell you of my plan:
I'm staying in my sterile bed
And never ever going out again.

SMELLY TRAINERS

We didn't pay too much for them -
These trainers we bought cheap -
But after six months loyal service
They didn't smell so sweet.
We took them to the doctors,
Showed them to the vets:
"Prognosis is not good" they said,
"We fear there'll soon be death."
It cannot be, we cried,
We simply will not listen!
The medics shook their heads
"You try sniffin' them."
We did and we passed out....
The stench of rotting trainers -
We decided we should shoot them:
Well who can really blame us?
We held a torchlight service
And prayed for both their soles,
Each trainer had one last request
Before the bullet holes.
Oh please have mercy on our soles,
We heard the trainers plead,
Put us through the washing machine:
We promise we'll go clean!
The shoes they ran on program one -
A must for heavy soiling -
The soap and bubbles frothing round
And the water nearly boiling.
We added cleaner and lemon juice
Then hung them out to dry
In the terrible heat of the midday sun -
What an awful way to die.

But the trainers were still breathing
Lying face down on their belly;
We shuddered as we breathed in
But the trainers were not smelly.
'Tis true they had shrunk a little
But the trainers still fit well:
'Tis wise to pause with sweaty soles
Before condemning them to hell.

THE DEN

It's our den,
You can't come in.
It's our secret,
You can't discover it.
It's not for grown-ups
Or kids not in our gang:
They do not know the code word
We will not let them in.
The roof is made of metal,
The walls are four strong sticks,
A polythene sheet makes good sound walls
Instead of building bricks.
And now we've made it comfortable
With a borrowed rug or two,
And soon a little bed in there
To stay the whole night through.
But what about the darkness,
The scary black of night?
We haven't electricity
But we like a candle light.

JUMP

It was tall
It was slender
And its bark was green.
It was a sycamore but I imagined more
Or less - the long neck of a dinosaur.
The cold of a creature,
The features
Of a reptile,
And I sat on its head
And looked down for a mile.
I couldn't see his toes, I wanted a parachute.
Jump you chump, jump you chump
And if you didn't you were a useless lump,
A scaredy cat and all that
Goes with it like never being
Picked for football and cricket.
Come on Brontosaurus brain!
I leap, let go of the head far behind.
I see no dinosaur toes.
I fall like a ball on the soft ground
And roll over and over and over again,
Away from the crushing of ten ton feet
Of the dinosaur on his policeman's beat.

THE BOY WHO FORGOT

This is the story of the boy who forgot,
Who was sent on an errand
And forgot what it was.
Who spent his time thinking
Of otherly plans
Instead of thinking of
The job in hand.
Send him to the kitchen -
He knows where he's been
But why he ever went there
Is a mystery to him.
Ask him where his school bag is
You'll receive a vacant look.
Ask him where his letters are
And his spellings book -
Or his money and his purse
The fleece he once was wearing
And you ask him where the fleece is now
Not a thing but his empty staring.
A problem with the laces
He forgets to tie them tight
Left sprawling on the pavement
Things just aren't quite right.
I've forgotten where my shoes are
Have you seen my coat?
The boy who drowns in a sea of lost
And never keeps afloat.
And me I'm sure it's catching
I know I'm just as bad
Forgetting names of people and places
The boy has driven me mad.

Yes, this is the boy
Whose name I've forgotten -
Could be any eight year old
To qualify for this poem.

BATHTIME RULES

Before bed
Comes bathtime, a good time:
Baths are not for bathing
But for swimming in.
Bubbles simply must abound:
Soap moustaches and beards
Shall be worn.
Water must be hand warm
And hair washing
Must not be done
Under any circumstances.
Half the water in the bath
Shall be splashed
On to the surrounding floor
And adults placed
In a room next door.
Not less than two
To take to the tub
And pulling the plug
Must be done
At intervals
Before end of bath
And beginning of bedtime -
A bad time!

BACKPACK*

Back pack
Is bad pack.
I'll kick and I'll scream
I'm not being in it.
I'll froth and I'll flay,
I'll fling and I'll fit.
Bite and shout
Take me out, let me out!
Yes backpack
He is bad pack.
And I'm a good girl
Yes a good girl.

* Babies and toddlers are often carried in backpacks by their parents

ICE-CREAM

Offer me olives,
Beg me to eat bread.
Special spaghetti,
Meat without the fat.
Salivate on salmon,
Chewing on ciabatta.
Tantalise me with tomato
And cheesy roast potato.
Fingers on the fish and chips,
Tomato sauce that sticks to lips,
And pick and choose the little bits -
Smear the rest across the bib.
I'm not impressed with what's on offer -
There must be sweet you have to proffer?
No cake, no chocolate no other dream,
All I want is my ice-cream.
Ice-cream, ice-cream, ice-cream,
White or brown or green,
But please, ice-cream;
Or I'll scream
Again and again
And again.

COCKROACH

Cockroach in your knickers -
It's not an idle threat.
I wait with the cockroach in my hand
You stand with bated breath.
I feel his feelers feeling
I see his cockroach grin
I imagine what he'll feel like
Crawling o'er your skin.
You scream at me
"You wouldn't do!"
And I reply I would.
"You couldn't do!" you challenge me
And I reply I could.
"Do it then!" you call my bluff
And I am moving in.
You realise that I'm not kidding
And turn and start to run.
I am chasing, you will lose
I know I am the faster
And now I have you in my grasp
I take the cockroach - "Down your pants!"
Er - now I've dropped a clanger,
Of the cockroach there's no sign,
Now I know he's not in yours
As I feel him crawl through mine.

MISSING DAD

We bury you last head
First feet
Leave you for dead.
Watch the Skegness seagulls swooping
Over your sandy tomb
And say our prayers
Before we leave you
Dead and buried
Under a tonne
Of wet Skegness sand.
About the sky
Clouds are gathering
Over the horizon
Tankers disappearing
And soon you won't be breathing
In the freezing
Skegness seaside air.

After tea I checked.
You had either risen from the dead
Or the Skegness seagulls
Took you for a ride.

THE WELL

Black
And
Wet
Is
The water in
The well,
But when we drew the water
The bucket had a different tale to tell.
Emerging into Heaven's light
The bucket full of water bright.
Blue
Is
The sky
O'er
The well
Well, well, well, well
You can never ever ever tell.

SHOUTS

Shouts out in the playground
Communicating sound.
Shouts awake, awake
You'll be late, late, late.
Shout out loud in sleep
To escape a bad dream.
Shout out at your play
Tag the one who got away
Shout at me in anger
A warning shout approaching danger.
And shouts for the madman
Inside his head.
In the mouths of the dumb
Murmurs made instead.
And the ears of the deaf
Would welcome a shout
And the child in a coma
Shouts to get out.
And a shout in space
Is a nothing sound.

SEASIDE

Across the rocks
Yellow hanging blocks
Lies the sea
Bubbles, blue and green.
Over the ocean sky
Skater clouds by and by.
Beneath the waves
Mermaid caves.
Above the sky
The other side.
Upon my face
This mystical place.
And in my mind
Another kind.

WEED

A wind whistled, kept me awake.
In the morning seaweed waited whilst
Tons more wanted to come ashore.
A brown slick of ragged ribbon
Tugged from the seabed by
The hand of a storm.
An odour of ocean
As we step on the sponge.
They say this stuff is mermaids' hair -
I say there's a lot of bald mermaids
Out there.

THE MUSEUM (AND THE FAT CONTROLLER)

We ignored the sign on the gate which read
"Trespassers will be prosecuted, hung or shot for dead".
We smiled at the sign for security cameras
And wondered what pictures they'd take of us.
The miniature line under six foot of grass -
We're shaking our heads at the terrible mess
And creeping about making new approaches
Novel angles on ancient coaches,
Whose tattered seats are tired and torn
From ghostly passengers long since gone;
Whose windows are broken by vandals' stone
Left by their engines to die all alone.
After several attempts we are into the shed,
But the shed is alone and the engines have left.
There's no steam, no diesel, or so it appears
There hasn't been any for quite a few years.
No ancient engines just old black lines
And a dark empty shed a sign of the times.
"They've been taken away, they are hiding elsewhere,"
Said a bowler hat man who appeared from nowhere.
We're pleased to hear the engines aren't lost
"I'm pleased you're pleased" said the friendly old ghost.
We left for the sun and security cameras;
Hoped that the man from the shed would follow us -
We'd love our picture taken with the man in the bowler:
The ghostly image of the Fat Controller.

BERT GOES BANG

Our cousin Bert
Was a greedy little git.
Whenever there was chocolate found
Bert would want his bit.
Even if it wasn't his
He'd still demand a piece,
And if you asked some in return
He'd smile at you and wink
And say I'm sorry I've got no chocolate today.
But we knew that he had
Kept it in his anorak pocket
Deep in the dark of a dungeon pocket.
So I decided I'd put an end to it.
My thirty best friends I gathered around
And with Bert in tow we hit the town.
We bought up all the chocolate there
And Bert he asked for his fair share.
We gave it to him, five kilos in his hand,
And Bert ate the lot and began to expand
And expand and expand....
Then we all stood back and waited for the bang.
Bang went Bert, bang went Bert,
It's OK, he isn't hurt.
It seems he's just a different Bert.
He looked kind of different
A long trail of liquid,
Brown, with bits of blue anorak
And Bert left floating in it.

CAR SICK

Mam I don't feel very well.
Well stop your wriggling
And stare straight ahead.
(I hadn't been moving
But you can't tell Mam nothing)
And take your head out of that wretched comic.
(But the comic lay with my bottom upon it)
I am staring straight ahead and I'm not reading
Tut tut, she tutted - Mam never believed me.
Mam I really feel ill....
Well hold your stomach in
And try thinking nice thoughts
Of feeling well again.
It's mind over matter
Your mind's getting weaker -
And you should stare straight ahead
(I hadn't moved my head since
The last time she'd said)
Mam I really think I'm going to be ill.
That's it, she shouted,
I don't want to hear no more of it!
Dad said nothing, Mam did all the talking.
Dad stared straight ahead
Did just as Mam said.
Your Dad has to concentrate -
Don't disturb his train of thought.
Do you want an accident, do you want us all dead?
(No, she replied for me,)
Well then stare straight head!
Mam I think this time I'm going to be sick -
I stared straight ahead -
And let 'em have it, every bit!

DOUBLE DECKER

On the top of a double-decker
There's really lots of fun,
Looking out of dirty windows
We pull faces at everyone.
Grinning at the bus conductor
With his whirring ticket machine:
He wears a smart black uniform
And his brilliant badge it gleams.
Passengers choke on cigarette smoke
But nobody seems to complain,
And the fog forms thick on the upper deck
As the sodden raincoats steam.
Big boys make for the back of the bus,
Laugh loud and scream and shout,
But only when the coast is clear -
Watch out, the conductor's about!
Now I can't tell you what's so special
About a double-decker,
But I NEVER sit on the lower deck
On the upper it's much better.

GIRL ON A SWING

Girl on a swing
She ought to know better
Than to swing on a swing
After bread and butter.
Girl on a swing
She wants to go faster.
Girl on a swing
She wants to climb higher
With the wind in her hair
And the feeling in her tummy
Swings the girl on a swing
Back and forth
Up and down
Sees the sights
From the height of her swing.
Girl on a swing
Head in the clouds
Touches the sky
Smiles at the sun.
Shining on the girl on a swing
And perhaps she does know better
Than to spoil her fun
Over a piece of bread and butter.

JUNGLE SWING

You should try the jungle swing
Your mate can push you
You're a wild thing.
You could be on an aeroplane
You could be a rocket
Engines in your undies
No way that you can stop it.
Yeah - out there in the jungle
All the apes are having fun
I tell you that it's evolution
And it's only just begun -
We'll be jungle-swinging everywhere
It's the movement for the future
So get yourself a learnin'
Forget your old computer.
Forget the literacy hour
All the maths you did in school
From now on we'll be jungle-swinging
'Cos jungle-swinging's cool.

COOL

Cool is the climate inside my fridge
Not the music I like
Or the words I speak,
What the labels say on the bum of my jeans,
The fashion I wear, the games I play
Or the friends I keep and enemies I make.
It's not what I eat or the places I'm seen
The fat or the thin or the build in between.
A beauty they didn't give to my face -
There must be a last in the egg and spoon race
I listen to what you all have to say
I go home, sleep on it, go my own way.
Yes cool is the way some people behave
And I'm not one of them - but I make
Up my own mind on
What is wrong and what is right
For me.

SCHOOL TRIP

Mr. Kay leads the kids' crocodile
On the faithful old coach
Not a tear in his eye
Mr. Kay waves goodbye
And hello to the day ahead
To no more pupils, rest instead.
We have fought for prime places,
The back seat where you can wave
At confused car drivers
Whose gaze tries so hard to avoid ours.
They, the teachers, had given us worksheets
But we're not interested
Preferring songs and sweets
The ruder the song the better
And somewhere around the eighth verse we're told off
By a very red-faced teacher.
The sicklier the sweet the better.
Ten minutes after the first lurch of gear change
From Greasy Ken (looks like our dads) the driver
We are busy undoing every wrapper.
Squashing, shovelling, push the chocolate, fit it in.
Crunch, crack the Trebor boiled sweet, teeth are breaking.
Someone (a young teacher who looks a bit like our sisters) yells
We're nearly in Llangollen
And shocking, we hadn't noticed the country rolling by
Between toffee, nougat and giant size bites.
We'll be at the castle soon, she begins again.
Teachers take the crocodile across the moat
And of course, we try to shove one another in, with no-one looking.
We'd dream of boiling tar and arrows from on high
And say out loud in a threatening way
"Watch it Willy or we'll load you in the cannon"
And just when Willy's about to start crying, we start laughing.

Then he's smiling, he sort of knows we're joking.
Right, start writing, and there's nail-biting and staring.
We haven't been listening so
We make up a lot of stuff about kings and medieval fighting
Fill a page to keep them happy, back on the bus
For a spot of lunch.
Several castles later and an old wreck of an abbey
We're back on our homeward journey.
Bought extra supplies instead of boring tourist guides.
Chocolate abounds, fizzy pop, up and down Welsh mountains.
Another accident I was the first to see in front of me.
A great eruption another school trip session of chucking
And the sick moves downstream as the bus is lurching
Uphill, "Miss Davies, Shaun's been ill!"
Another and another. Final toll of five.
The driver complains of the stench, we're quite used to it.
Mr. Kay greets us holding a mop and bucket.
Better than last year Mr. Kay, no deaths
A little less sickness. The crocodile disembarks.
I'm monitor I have to mop and afterwards Mr. Kay
Asks did I enjoy it - he means not the sick
But the school trip. Mr. Kay, I wouldn't be without it!

MRS. BOTTOMLEY

Class, your new teacher, Mrs. Bottomley.
Strange sort of name, I'm sure you'll agree,
And me, I sniggered quite naturally.
"Please do tell us what you find so funny?"
But I didn't couldn't wouldn't dare
Face Mrs. Bottomley; it wasn't fair
To have her call herself such a name -
Not me but her bottom that was to blame.

SUNDAY NIGHT

Sunday night and you
Won't catch me.
Sunday night and
I'm far away
From the Sunday bath
And the back-to-school
And the Monday
Early morning call.
In bed by seven
Is the Sunday rule
Up bright and early
For the Monday morning school.
But bed at seven
Is a waste of time
When you could be having fun
Staying out till nine.
So I slipped out
Of the house tonight
No bath or early bed
I've got it right.
Down in the woods
Hiding in the den
For a late start on Monday.
I'll be back at ten!

OUR STREET

Our street (or rather cul-de-sac),
A monument to the games children play
In hot and cold, sun and rain;
With an all-weather tarmac surface
Ideal for pursuit of childhood pleasures,
Washable chalk marks for tennis and cricket
String for the net, wooden box for the wicket.
Garden wall for the boundaries, lawns for the sixes
To anger the neighbours of crimson faces,
Who respond to the football smashing their roses
By sending it back with a pin prick hole in it.
They were our gates for the goals,
Our string, our rackets and bats and balls,
Our roller skates, us mad on bikes:
Our playful, inventive minds.
I'd like to remember it as it was,
Full of kids and the deafening noise
Of joy.

LINING UP

They'll never pick me
Too fat and dumb.
Too "when-the-ball's-passed-to-me
Where-do-I-run?"
Which goal are we shooting on?
And when I stand
I stand stiff in the mud
The ball: thump! In the stomach.
Through the tears I laugh
Then cry, I guess that's why
You won't pick me
And I'm left last in line.
But there comes a time
When you must choose
And thinking you have everything to lose.
Instead I won the day, a ricochet,
All oblivion, an inadvertent
Header
Straight past their goalkeeper.
When I come around,
They're proud
And pleased
To choose me.

TEA WITH AUNTIE

Not my real Auntie -
Said she wouldn't stand any hanky-panky
And what's wrong with ham in ye
Sandwiches you ungrateful lump?
We ought to dump
You in deepest darkest Africa
Where people eat leaves,
And you, you haven't a care
Wipe that smile off your face!
I'm serious, I'll put a grimace in its place!
Dream, dream - there's no ice cream
For nasty twerps
With naughty burps
And the manners of a dustbin man.
Look at you, I'll tell your Mam!
No Auntie, we'll be good
Everything Auntie you say - we know we should.
We'll eat a pig,
We won't want ice-cream
To wash it down with.
We'll send the money to those kids
So they won't have to eat leaves.
We won't laugh when you're serious
And if we're tempted,
We'll bite our cheeks so hard
We won't mind about the bloody mess.
As regards the washing up
You never need lift a finger,
And we'll sweep and clean and walk the dog
And try not to tread on Ginger
- Your favourite cat.

All of this and more of that
We will do for thee,
Oh, our favourite Auntie:
Enrol us at the school of slavery!
We admire your diligence and bravery
In keeping this our little secret
And not telling mother the tiniest
Bit of it.

WOODCHURCH BATHS

The baths have a deep end
For people to drown in if they can't swim.
There are cartoons on the wall
Showing what you can't do -
Like petting or ducking and pushing
People in the pool.
These are known as The Rules.
Lifeguards blow whistles, chase you out
If you play the fool.
I keep to the shallow end and duck myself;
Sometimes I throw myself in, but I don't jump.
Keith Sherlock caught a lump
On his foot.
We said he'd have to have it chopped off.
We were dropped off
At the baths by a number 19 bus
And both of us,
My brother and me,
Were given money
For an entrance fee and bags of crisps
'Cos swimming can leave you feeling weak,
Said Mum, who knew
About medical things and what to do.
We swim, we're on our way
To catch the bus home
When a house brick is thrown
From on high through a window:
It's time to run!
No questions asked.
They've begun
The attack on our money.

We're out of sight
Safe at the shops
Buy what we like
Catch the bus home.
We don't tell Mum,
She always knows
She says
People in Council houses shouldn't throw stones.

OLD AND NEW

Five four three two one
Thunderbirds alas have gone
But keep coming back
Again and again and again.
It seems we cannot get enough of Brains,
Of mid-flight bombings, accidents on trains.
Calling International Rescue! Calling International Rescue!
Why didn't they make more episodes of you?
Of Virgil, Gordon, Mr. Tracy,
Tin-Tin, Parker, Lady Penelope;
Of Thunderbird Five locked on to the sun
And John's waxy face beginning to run.
Calling International Rescue, do you read me?
And what have they left us on TV?
Pokémon -here today
Gone
Tomorrow.

SAM'S SOLO

Honing his skill to the point of precision,
Sam kept in mind an extraordinary vision
Of Sam about to take on them all
With practice in the park and at home against the wall.
Sam knew he was ready by the middle of May;
Wouldn't tell his team mates, didn't want to say
That he Sam would go it all alone,
They'd stand back and admire, they wouldn't have to run.
Midway through the first he hung back for the break.
It wasn't quite the moment he'd simply lie in wait.
And sure enough it happened a fair few minutes on
He collected the ball at the half way line and ran and ran and ran
Past one, past two, past three, past four -
Surely Sam was going to score
The greatest solo of the season
Only goalie to beat but for some reason
Sam was looking at an empty net
Ceremoniously he buried the ball in it.
He ran and dived like they did on the TV
And expected his colleagues to hug and kiss him.
Sam looked up, there was no-one about.
Sam's manager waved and gave him a shout.
"Good solo Sam you've beaten the lot!
Only one problem as the ball crossed the line
We were enjoying a rest at half time!"

HOLIDAYS

An army slow in summer long
Moves on and on
To the green grass stadium.
And sporty soldiers
Take their guard;
Batter wooden stakes in ground
Made cement by drought.
Birds whisper warnings,
And silence -
Save the mower speaks.
Fielders take the field.
Hayfever sufferers sneeze,
Stifled in white handkerchiefs.
Come and go -
Failures, heroes
Big-hitters, ticklers, ducks,
Near misses,
Big time squash-drinkers,
Bowlers,
Big-mitted wicket keepers
Hit, run
Till the dusk comes.
Marching on, marching on
The army coming home,
Coming home.
Their flag is flown
For another holiday.

MY SHEET

My sheet, I cling to it
With its soft cotton embrace.
Covers you with kisses
From toes to face.
A safe and snug place
To hide from anger and doubt
That lies without
On the other side of my sheet
Where weary walk
The troubled feet
Of another race
Who have no sheet, no snug place.
After a warm soak
I wrap myself in sheet and cloak
And cannot describe the peace within.
Where does the sheet end and I begin?

IT SHOULD HAVE BEEN POSTPONED

It should have been postponed.
I knew that when David Burley
Fell over twice in the warm-up,
Said it was muddy,
Said that his mummy
Didn't take kindly
To washing his kit.
She wasn't a machine
And why should she do it
When the bloomin' games teacher
Ought to know better
Than let the kids play football
In this sodden weather?
It should have been postponed
Judging by the frown
On the face of Mrs. Brown
Who always rolled her son an apple
For good luck
To ward off fierce strikers
With him stuck
Between the two posts.
He alone stood tall amidst a defence which boasts
The worst record in the division
"And it would be worse if it wasn't
For my son's goal keeping precision"
Said Mrs. Brown,
And she threw her bag down
In disgust
And had to run past us
To reach her son
With the apple of her eye.

It should have been postponed
When we went in 1-0 down at half time
And the mud in our muscles meant
We couldn't run
And the wet in our bones
Seemed to spoil all the fun
And we knew the other team had won.

It should have been postponed
When we went in 8-0 down at full time.

SWEETS

A jar of sweets
A jar of treats
Have you anything for a penny?
For me who doesn't have much money
Just an Anglo Bubbly
Or a chewy toffee
Or Jap Dessert, Liquorice Torpedo
Everton Mint or Chocolate Rolo
Or Rhubarb and Custard.
Suck a Pear Drop
Eclair I'd declare
I'll eat the lot
And more and more and more ...
But I spent it all in the toy shop
Next door.

BISCUIT BARREL

Who's been at the biscuits?
It was not I
Who picked out all the chocolate ones
And left the rest to die.
Who's been at the biscuits?
There's only plain ones left.
Who's nibbled all the nice bits?
Who's the icing thief?
Who's been in the biscuits?
Let me see your mitts....
I don't know how it got there
But the chocolate lay in bits
Upon the palm of my hand,
So she knew I was the one
Who'd been at the biscuits
'Cos biscuit-eating's fun!

MR. LADYMAN

A grown-up in his twenties;
Looked like a man who spent
All day parading around universities
And we all bet that he secretly wore glasses
Like the swats who always came top
Of our classes.
He treats us like real kids,
Talks to us like half wits,
Moves his mouth like a fish
So we can't mistake the words
Coming out of it.
We're not from the deaf and dumb
School mister
We can hear yer!
Fishy begins to gabble.
"Fine day for togger!"
Togger? What's togger you daft bogger?
And we snigger
I haven't the heart to tell him it's soccer - not togger;
That's a poofter's game - like rugger.
"Well come along matey -
Pass the ball!"
And Murph reluctantly chucks it
From his space inside the goal
He's awkward with a ball
Doesn't suit him at all.
Better with a quill pen
Writing things down again and again and again....
"Let's have a shot!"
He toe-ends it screaming past us lot
And over the Bottomley's garden gates
Where, past experience tells us,
A pin and the death of a football awaits.

This grown-up wise and grown-up clever!
Well he might be, Mr. University,
But take a lesson from us: never, never
Use the toe, always the side of a football shoe.

DISCIPLINE

Miss Williams wanted a milk monitor,
We all pretended we liked writing stories
And buried our heads in our English books
And ignored her.
"Not one volunteer not one itsy-bitsy helper?"
A stunned silence greeted her.
"We'll see about this, yes we shall see."
And there was something about the way
Miss Williams said her S's that told us
Miss Williams was more than a little angry.
The next day she walked straight into our
Classroom and instead of the Register
Showed us a tiny revolver.
"See this?" (we certainly did) "I'm going
To give each one of you a closer look,
Ask you a question and yes it's loaded".
We shivered; Miss Williams wandered
From desk to desk and pointed the
Gun at each one of us.
"Do you want to be milk monitor?"
Without a doubt, some terrific nodding here
Even if our voices gave out through fear
And terror took to every bone,
Yes, Miss Williams, yes I will never leave you alone
And make you move the milk about on your own.
It was too much for Kenneth Johnson
Who broke down in tears at the sight
Of Miss Williams, guns and bullets
Not a nod, not a whisper, Kenneth was finished.
"Good, Class 5, good".

We never saw the gun again
And everyone was too scared to report Miss Williams
To the headmaster who would have sided with her.
Class 5 has 32 pupils and 31 milk monitors.
Kenneth Johnson never recovered
From the shock.

ANIMALS AND CHILDREN

Children all love furry animals
This is a known fact.
That's why my mate Jacko and me
Decided we'd buy a rat.
We were fed up of fluffy bunnies
And a short or long haired cat.
We like the pinky flesh of a scary tail
And two beady eyes of our rat.
We decided we'd call him Gnasher
He was tough and lean and mean
He'd leap at your throat from a distance
And tear you apart at the seams.
He sharpened his teeth every morning
He filed his nails at night
He worked on his biceps during the day
He was spoiling for a fight.
I showed him pictures of sewers
Where his hardest mates hung out
I told him one day he'd act as hard
I told him what rat life was really about.
We told him he wasn't a bunny
We told him that rats weren't nice
They had hard skins as tough as old boots
And cold hearts as freezing as ice.
We thought we'd taught him everything
He was ready for the test
A visit to our pet open day
To be showed off at school with the rest.

But guess what happened to Gnasher
When he showed up in a cage at our school?
He suddenly turned all furry on us
And the kids said that Gnasher was cool.
The kids said:-
We've never wanted to pet a rat
But Gnasher's so cuddly and fluffy
Can we take him home this weekend?
You might have him back on Monday.

POCKET MONEY

They said they'd give me pocket money
When I reached the age of eight,
So here I am with my pockets ready
You can fill them while I wait.
They give me one or two coins
With the promise of more next week.
How long will it take to fill these pockets?
A year or so at this rate.
I'll tell you about pocket money,
Something that I found out
It's not for buying pockets with
You can buy just what you like!
I'll tell you another secret -
You don't store money in pockets
You either spend it down the toy shop
Or in a special money box-it!

TWO PENGUIN BISCUITS

Two Penguin biscuits
Each has a wrapper
One gold, one green
Colour shouldn't matter.
Two Penguin biscuits
With gold or green wrapper
But the choice that you make
Does seem to matter.
Two Penguin biscuits
What's wrong with the wrapper?
It's not gold it's green
And to my mind it matters.
Two Penguin biscuits
It doesn't matter -
There's chocolate hiding
Beneath the wrapper.
Two Penguins biscuits
I want the gold wrapper
It's the colour that counts
Not the chocolate that matters.
Two Penguin biscuits
I won't have the green
I don't care for the chocolate
That's sandwiched between.
One Penguin biscuit
It doesn't matter
But I'll eat the biscuit -
You chew the wrapper.

LIKE ME THE WAY I AM

You were nasty,
Pinched me hard,
Wouldn't let me join in
Your games in the playground.
Told lies about me,
Ganged up on me,
Made me lonely,
Laughed at me
So that I never want to see you
Or ever go to school again.
You turned the world against me
And I did nothing wrong
Except for being myself.
You didn't like that,
And everyone else who
Doesn't like me
The way I am
Has the same problem -
And it's yours.

DAFT DOG

Daft Dog just wagged his tail
That was all.
He couldn't speak
Just gave a woof.
He couldn't hear
His ears were fluff.
Wouldn't chase the cat around
Preferred to lie on solid ground
And sleep all of his life away
Dream of bones and Pal and Chunky.
We called him "Patch"
He answered to "Spot"
We told him why -
He asked us what?
I showed Daft Dog to all my mates
They couldn't believe my luck.
With a dog as lazy and stupid as he
There's no need to go out for a walk.

HOW TO HANDLE A BAD DREAM

Rule No.1
When having a bad dream
It's important to remember
The shadows you made up inside your head
Aren't real, like pictures on paper.

Rule No.2
But if you can't remember,
And the shadows are real like witches,
Then perhaps you would like to consider
One of the following switches:

Rule No.3
Switch to self control
And the baddies stop the chase.
You are rescued by lots of good goodies
With kind smiles and friendly face.

Rule No.4
If switch to self control won't work
Then press on the auto alarm.
Wake up and cuddle your pillow,
Breathe deeply until you are calm.

Rule No.5
If the auto alarm won't function,
Shout as loud as you can in your dream
And hope that your parents come running
At the terrible sound of your scream.

Rule No.6
If shouting turns to silence
Try to sleepwalk your way out of trouble
And find someone else to sleep next to
And give them a lovely warm cuddle.

MY WORLD

Where has all the good gone?
I don't see it in the news
Not on our television.
I hear
"Don't go out -
There are strangers about."
But I am introduced to strangers from time to time
Friends of my parents who smile
And prove themselves to be really rather kind.
We're told harm is all about us
And he is hiding in bushes
On lonely buses
In darkened lanes
In woods, watching from windows
Waiting to catch us.
But I say there is love all around us
And Nature can surprise us
As she puts a warm hand on our shoulder
And beckons us to come closer.
Whispers wonderful words
Of a truly loving world.
Oh sure there are problems -
We'd be the first to admit them -
But it's not like the world on television.
It's not about mostly bad men and women,
It's all about good guys
And helping and giving.
It's not about bad guys
And selfish and killing.

So we're going to have a
A new kind of vision
For all mankind and women
People hugging and greeting and kissing
A child returned who once went missing
People eating who once were starving
No more rich and poor only sharing
And young people caring.
And good news gets to grab the headlines.

CURE

Give me the soothing pink,
The syrup of Calpol,
A wondrous drink!
For fevers, aches and broken bones,
Colds and flu and runny nose,
TV eyes, earache, headache,
Sudden death, toothache, Calpol make
Heap big better when
You're under the weather.
Colour in the cheeks, a healthy glow
When before you looked like death warmed up
With cheeks as white as snow.
Down comes the pulse,
And the temperature too,
Now you can do
What you really want to do,
Like play out all day
With you mates in the park
Instead of lying half-dead
In your bed in the dark.
My parents are alternative
They take herbs and smells not pills;
But when it comes to curing me,
Calpol cures all ills.

THINGS THAT GO BUMP

Things that go
Bump in the night.
Ghosts and robbers
They give me a fright.
A squeaky floor
A creaking door
The heavy breathing
And someone screaming.
I can't see
In the scary black.
My heart in my mouth
I can't put it back!
Then all of a sudden
A terrible bump
And my brother has fallen
Out of the top bunk!

THE MERMAID

A miniature mermaid in a rock pool,
I found her hiding there
Underneath a forest of straggly seaweed
Making ribbons in her hair.

The sea was miles out from shore,
Had left her high and dry,
And as I bent a little lower
I heard the mermaid cry:

"I'm shrinking by the second
That's why I shed a tear.
If I stay here very much longer
I shall surely disappear."

"How is it I can help you?
What is it that you need?"
"I need the depths of yonder sea,
The food on which I feed."

I dipped fingers in the rock pool
And gently picked her out.
Strode on and on far out from shore
To where the waves they sing and shout.

And though the swell was high
And the water crashed on sand,
I gently let her out to sea
Just as she had planned.

Some years later, I sailed
Upon that self same sea
In a mighty craft full of precious cargo
Bound for the West Indies.

But a terrible storm it blew up
And washed me from the deck;
And I watched the ship sink 'fore my eyes
As I clung on to the wreck.

When I couldn't cling on much longer,
Not in that icy swell,
And the cloud of death came over me
And my body it was still.

My lungs were full of water,
My heart was full of pain.
I said my last goodbyes:
"I'll not see you again!"

Then just as I was finished,
I was hoisted from the ice
And carried miles to safety
To the shores of paradise.

The mermaid she had saved me
And bore me to the isle,
And set me down on the golden sand,
Left me with a smile.

She told me that for certain
One good turn deserves another,
And since I'd saved her life that day
I'd always be her brother.

A passenger steamer picked me up,
I found my way back home.
Now I always check in rock pools
For mermaids left alone.

GIVE ME MORE TOYS

Give me more toys!
I know I could borrow yours
But give me more toys
I'm losing track
Of the hundreds I have hidden in a cupboard stack.

Give me more toys!
The shiny and bright,
The ones that fire rockets, the ones that glow at night.

Give me more toys!
In fancy cardboard packets,
The one with screeching sirens, the one that makes a racket.
The one that talks when I press his chest,
The one they show on TV is currently the best.

Give me more toys!
I'm bored of these.
I want another Sega.
I want another computer.
I want what the boy down the street has got,
I want more than the lot of yer.

Give me more toys!
No I can't play outside,
I'm too busy getting tired of the toys you've yet to buy.

Give me more toys!
Yes I know they cost money
But am I not your darling boy, your flopsy little bunny?
So give me more toys
Yes more toys!

After all is said and done
Nothing could be finer
Than to fill our little home
With all the plastic made in China.

TANTRUM

This is tantrum, this is trouble
When "mine" is the only word I'm hearing
The legs are buckling at the knees
And the body's disappearing.
The two year old is lying prostrate
Kicking and screaming against ill fate
Which has dealt another unkindly blow
To this urchin, this unlucky so-and-so.
You try walking away from the scene
At first she stops then starts again
Only this time louder, more manic than before
A spinning top on the dirty floor.
She gives no answer or the answer is "no."
How to tame the animal in the zoo?
Ice cream, chocolate and biscuits won't do
There's only one option - I'll have a go!
And I do! I collapse in a heap on the ground
I'm no longer me but a flailing mound
Of helicopter arms and legs, a writhing mass of limbs
And an out-of-control wailing, a terrible din.
To passers-by I appear just another nutter
But *she* stops short in her tracks - I think that she knows better
You can't have your own father an embarrassing heap
Time to stop the tantrum get yourself back on your feet.

THE TALKING TURKEY DINOSAUR

Said ever so clearly to me
From his position in the middle
Of my plate -
Listen mate
Do us a favour don't eat me
I'm breadcrumb, I'm battered,
I'm cheap minced turkey.
Fatty I'll fool you to taste so good
I'm chemical extra synthetic food.
What's more, I don't roar
One hundred percent turkey, no dinosaur,
Not a bit, I'm sorry mate.
I'm a low class meal
With a high class name -
But they call me brontosaurus
So you'll eat me just the same.

TV KIDS

TV kids got their fingers on the button.
Without TV your life is worth nothing.
Analogue and digital, sure we got the lot
With wide screen and surround sound I'll tell you what -
At weekends, on school holidays, it's a good twelve hours a day
And we don't bother speaking to our parents, their noise gets in the way.
There's reports out in the papers, they say it's antisocial;
They say we cannot concentrate and study like we used to.
There's talk of us not able to amuse ourselves in play
Or communicate, express our thoughts in some intelligible way.
But I say - well I haven't got an opinion,
Sucked down the tube of my television.
Dad says the TV's killed me, I've been pronounced brain dead
And that I'm paying as I'm viewing but the cost is in my head;
Or I'm living a remote life and my mind has gone to bed
Gone to bed, gone to bed, gone to bed.

WATCHING THE RAIN

The legs dangle
And my hands fall to my heart;
I lean back,
Take to the dreamy black:
Each drop a fresh start
And a river tear to flow,
Take its course to finish
Flat out on the sill below,
Flat out on the sill above
I wink to check what
The weather is making.
More of rain
Rivers merge on this glass pane
And time continues its run
As I remain
Motionless
On a wet day
Watching and waiting....
Well, all for nothing
Save the quiet joy I'm feeling,
And I do believe
If the sunshine came
I would be left
Like the rain:
High and dry.

ROSA'S TOAD

'Twas to be a dark night for toad,
For hadn't he always been told
Never ever to step on the glassy black
Of the silky smooth tarmac road.
But when the evening rains came
Toad could not resist the call of the lane:
A chance to cross to the other side,
A new beginning, a new life;
More stones for hiding,
More insects for eating,
The glassy black tarmac to play on
And the whole night ahead of him.
Toad's eyes bulged even bigger,
His skin more slimy at the thought.
He hopped on the tarmac and back again:
He wasn't the risk-taking sort.
Off and on for half an hour,
Then he made a run
Back and forth and back and forth -
Taking a chance was fun!
I'll rest here a while, he thought to himself,
And hide from the morning sun....
Which alas for toad would never come,
His young toad life just begun:
He lay on the cool of the tarmac at night,
Dreamt of luxury life by the river,
And so died a happy contented toad
Under the wheels of a hit-and-run driver.

THE SUN AND THE MOON

When the sun drops below the horizon
And he tries to get some sleep,
Imagine his irritability
With that metabolic heat.
I think of his relief
When he climbs back in the sky,
And cools himself in the passing breeze
Whilst burning you and I.
I wouldn't like to be the sun,
I'd rather be the moon
Smiling there in the clear cool heavens,
Or wrapped in a cloudy cocoon.

NOT FOR ME (ABBEY)

They're trying me with a million spices,
They say it goes well with basmati rice, yes -
But no, I cannot quite agree:
The spice of life is not for me.
They're trying me with the veggie trick
"You don't eat these you'll end up sick
Your blood will turn bad, you'll run out of breath
Next time you scratch, you'll be bleeding to death."
Then there's the line "You've eaten this before -
Do us all a favour how about once more?"
But that was different I felt different then
The way I'm feeling now I can't eat the stuff again.
"You ate it round at so and so's
Her mother said, oh yes, we know...."
I should have know she'd blow my cover
Telling foody secrets to my secretive mother.
"Well, come on, don't hang about
Do you want to hear me scream and shout?
Tell her, Dad, she's got to eat her pasta."
"Oh yes" says Dad "or there'll be nothing after."
No more excuses, no more lies,
Here I am with my "pasta surprise":
Move that jaw and close those eyes,
Keep your mind on the sweetie prize.
It took 55 minutes to finish my meal.
"At last," cried Mother "I'm nearly asleep."
You promised, you promised, you promised me sweet!
"I hardly think you deserve a treat."
But the sweetie found its way on to my plate:
I smiled at my mother, the world was a great place.
It took 35 seconds to finish chocolate treat.
Why do we have a first course, I'll just make do with sweet!

WHAT DO BABIES DO?

Professors study
What do babies do.
Well my baby sister
Does lots of poo
And wee and cries
And eats a bit
Then drinks and burps
And then lets rip.
She crawls and tries
But cannot walk.
She points and gurgles
But cannot talk.
Rides in a pram
Has a morning kip
Then plays with her toys
Before her long night's sleep.
So if professor
You need a clue
Just ask my sister
What babies do.

WHAT DOES GOD DO FOR A JOB?

When He had finished creating the world
God said to Himself, "I've had enough"
And made himself unemployed.
"I'll sit back and rest on my fluffy white clouds
Play chess with the angels
Hide from the crowds.
I'm not in the habit of homework
I'm not looking for a career
I'm not moving to look for work
I'm God, I'm staying right here.
The angels tell me I'm lazy
That I lack a competitive streak
That I should have taken my SATs by now
With a view to my GCSEs.
(You know the trouble with you God
You sit there and waste your time thinking
Whilst others are working harder than you
And the jobs they are disappearing.)"
So God took a look in the newspaper
To see what he might like to be
The school he might like to attend
The subjects he needed to study.
"It's no good," says God, "this is not for me:
I don't really want to be working
I'd just as soon sit here and be."
We tried, said the angels
We cannot do more
I'm afraid you're a failure God, they said
You'll end up jobless and poor.
"Say what you like," said God,
"The thinking life is for me
Now you run along with the rest of the world
And waste your time being busy."

"You see," said God, "there's been a mistake:
When I invented the human being
I thought he might spend some of his time
Simply thinking and not always doing."

THE ANGELS BOUGHT GOD A NEW COLOURING BOOK

The angels bought God
A new colouring book.
At first it was OK
The sky was red at night
Or sometimes in the morning
And sheep were happy or sad depending.
People were black or white
Or a little bit yellow
And there were always new flowers
For God to get to work on.
Then I woke one morning
To see purple in the mirror
And a dark green dog
Chasing a light blue cat.
At school people were mostly purple
(Some a little indigo)
And school dinner
Was all off-yellow.
At games the grass was black
And red rain fell during the second half
Now it's night
And the sky is orange
With pretty pink clouds
To please the girls.
I'm praying, please God
Give up painting -
Or at least come along
To our art class tomorrow!

TRUTH

Today I watched open mouthed as
A cactus ate two smooth pine cones.
This morning I was told there are two
Suns in the sky: one of them hides.
And for elevenses I was given a nice pot of tea
Made exclusively from a proprietary indoor compost.
Fishes have been discovered in the toilet
And there is a mouse, name of Mickey, residing in our
backpack.
Everyday I am allowed invisible chocolate
Which fails to fill me up.
Kiwi fruits have turned into frogs
And we adults are becoming railway carriages.
So to bed but beware! You share
The same with dinosaurs.

This is a poem about Rosa who is aged two and has a very good imagination!

BIG TREE

Heap
Big tree
With
Heap
Big knees.
Hear the
Cheep cheep cheep
Of
Little birdies
Hiding in
A
Thousand leaves.
Please please
Save our trees
And his knees
And the birdies
And the leaves
And not forgetting
The honey bees.
If you like all of these
Don't chop them down - go plant a tree!

THE SONGS

THE GREAT SWEETSHOP ROBBERY

Ian Adams agreed with it -
Sweet shop owners had more than they needed.
We should set our little plan in motion:
The greatest sweetie redistribution.

Monday to Friday after school
We'd meet for manoeuvres as a rule.
We'd need to get the moves just right:
We'd want to win without a fight.

We needed a line or two to say
To help us robbers get our way:
We practised and practised and practised our song -
If you want justice - sing along:

Hold your hands up!
Get your chocolate out!
Don't want to hear anyone
Scream or shout.
Hey mister, what is this all about?
It's a genuine sweet shop robbery
Your Mars, your Twix, your Snickers
All for me, yeah, yeah, yeah, yeaah
All for me, yeah, yeah, yeah, yeaah
All for me!

The day it came and we left our den;
Stood inside the shop, two grown men
Each with a moustache and a fluffy beard -
I tell you we were looking weird.

Say mister - yeah, say mister - yeah,
This is a real gun!
We want all your sweeties:
We want to have some fun!

Hold your hands up!
Get your chocolate out!
Don't want to hear anyone
Scream or shout.
Hey mister, what is this all about?
It's a genuine sweet shop robbery
Your Mars, your Twix, your Snickers
All for me, yeah, yeah, yeah, yeaah
All for me, yeah, yeah, yeah, yeaah
All for me!

But Mr. Bateson - he was nobody's fool
Says "Kids your just not acting cool!
I know exactly who you are underneath that disguise
Now run home to mummy with your plastic gunny
Before I split my sides!

But before you do - sing your song.
I just love to sing along ...."

Hold your hands up!
Get your chocolate out!
Don't want to hear anyone
Scream or shout.
Hey mister, what is this all about?
It's a genuine sweet shop robbery
Your Mars, your Twix, your Snickers
All for me, yeah, yeah, yeah, yeaah
All for me, yeah, yeah, yeah, yeaah
All for me!

CHOCOLATÉ!
*(Pronounced "Chocolatay" - Spanish for chocolate.
The chorus is sung to the well-known song "La Cucaracha")*

Any size or any shape,
Chocolate made for me:
And when I'm eating chocolate
I sing this song you see:

(1-2, 1-2-3-)
Chocolat-ay! chocolat-ay! chocolatay para mi,
Si, chocolat-ay, chocolat-ay, chocolatay para mi,
cha-cha-cha!

Try me with the dark,
Give me the milk;
Rough and ready cooking chocolate
Or Galaxy smooth silk.

Chocolate full of almonds
A nut in every bite;
Give me heavy chocolate, man,
Or Aero chocolate light.

Chocolate with the coconut,
Chocolate with the mallow,
Or how about a toffee filling
You suck to death before you swallow.

I buy it from our sweet shop,
I purchase it abroad;
It doesn't matter where you are,
For chocolate, just one word:

(1-2, 1-2-3-)
Chocolat-ay! chocolat-ay! chocolatay para mi,
Si, chocolat-ay, chocolat-ay, chocolatay para mi,
cha-cha-cha!

Chocolate in the playground,
Chocolate back at home;
Chocolate breakfast, lunch and dinner
And often in between.

Chocolate in good company,
Chocolate on its own,
Chocolate under bedclothes
Tucked up in bed alone.

(1-2, 1-2-3-)
Chocolat-ay! chocolat-ay! chocolatay para mi,
Si, chocolat-ay, chocolat-ay, chocolatay para mi,
cha-cha-cha!

Chocolate whilst I'm living,
Chocolate till I die;
And afterwards in Heaven
In a chocolate laden sky.

Yes choco-late in this life
And chocolate in the next:
As long as there is chocolate
You can do without the rest!

(continued over page)

(1-2, 1-2-3-)
Chocolat-ay! chocolat-ay! chocolatay para mi,
Si, chocolat-ay, chocolat-ay, chocolatay para mi,
cha-cha-cha!

Chocolate for the Muslims
For Christians and all;
Don't bother with religion;
Come share a Chocolate Ball.

Yes, chocolate will save mankind
If there is a nuclear war:
Someone somewhere in a bunker
Lives on chocolate bars.

(1-2, 1-2-3-)
Chocolat-ay! chocolat-ay! chocolatay para mi,
Si, chocolat-ay, chocolat-ay, chocolatay para mi,
cha-cha-cha!

THE BOGEY MAN
(To the tune of "The Muffin Man")

I think I've seen the bogey man,
The bogey man, the bogey man;
I think I've seen the bogey man:
He lives in Ludham town.

I think I've seen the bogey man,
The bogey man, the bogey man;
I think I've seen the bogey man:
He lives inside our house.

I think I've seen the bogey man,
The bogey man, the bogey man;
I think I've seen the bogey man:
He sits upon our couch.

Oh guess who is the bogey man,
The bogey man, the bogey man;
Oh guess who is the bogey man:
I guess he is my dad.

He picks his nose, thinks I can't see,
Thinks I can't see, thinks I can't see;
He picks his nose, thinks I can't see
The green upon his hand.

And your Dad's are all bogey men,
They're bogey men, they're bogey men;
Yes your Dad's are all bogey men
In this grown-up bogey land!

GO TEDDY!

Sez Teddy to me, You know my life it's not right:
I'm sleepin' all da day an' I'm sleepin' all da night;
I've gotta move out to where da future's bright
Under da glare of da Disco-light!

I said, Go!
Go, Teddy, go go go!
Yo, Teddy, yo yo yo!
Go, Teddy, go go go!
Yo, Teddy, yo yo yo!
Yo, Teddy, yo!

Sez me to Teddy, Well, ya gotta look da part:
Ya gotta look cooool an' ya gotta look smart;
Ya need da sunglasses an' da shiny suit;
Ya need da tight trousers an' da cowboy boots!

I said, Go! etc.

Well, Teddy he's out dere a-struttin' his stuff,
Lookin' like da Teddy de chicks love to love;
But da bouncer here, he looks mean an' tough,
Looks at Teddy full of envy: he's had about enough.

I said, Go! etc.

Saez bouncer to me Teddy, well ain't you da one;
If you know what's good, you'll take my advice Son
Go back to your picnic, have some teddy-bear fun,
And leave these lovely ladies - now let's be movin' on!

I said, Go! etc.

Well, Teddy wasn't one to take his advice:
He didn't like da bouncer - no, da bouncer wasn't nice!
Da next thing I knew dere was a terrible clout:
One paw from Teddy an' da bouncer he was out!

I said, Go! etc.

So every Friday night he is da King o' da Club
His only bear necessity is buffin' his fluff!
Forget da honey, baby, I'm not Winnie DaPooh:
No, a bear's gotta dance, that's what a bear's gotta do!

I said, Go! etc.

POO ON YOUR SHOE

When you're out on the street
Keep a watch on your feet...
What you gonna do
About the - poo on
Your shoe?

When you're running down the road
Check out the brown load...
What you gonna do
About the - poo on
Your shoe?

When you're keeping goal
Keep an eye on your sole...
What you gonna do
About the - poo on
Your shoe?

When you're home again
Don't let the carpet stain.
Parents mad at you,
Tell them it's not true,
Some dog, somewhere else
Put the poo on your shoe.

(SING GOSPEL STYLE)
Ah-1-2, ah1-2-3-4
What you gonna do about the
Poo on your shoe?
DOO-DOO-DOO-DOO
Poo on your shoe?
DOO-DOO-DOO-DOO
Poo on your shoe?
DOO-DOO-DOO
What you gonna do about the
Poo on your shoe?
The poo, poo, poo on your shoe.
(REPEAT ABOVE AN OCTAVE UP THEN FINISH BELOW)
The poo, poo, poo *(VERY SLOW)*
O-ONNNNN
YOUR SHOE-OOOOOOOOOOOOOOOOO!

(Thank you and goodnight!)

BIMBO* RULES THE WORLD

Now you can eat Bimbo
Wherever you like;
You can eat it in the day,
You can eat it late at night;
And every time you're chewing
On this tasteless bread,
The ad man's words
Go around in your head:

Bimbo, Bimbo, Bimbo we love Bimbo!
Bimbo, Bimbo, Bimbo es mejor!

Bimbo au chocolat,
Bimbo plain pan;
You can't get away from this Bimbo, man!
There's Bimbo in the supermarket,
Bimbo on TV;
Bimbo on the billboard poster
Staring back at me.

Bimbo, Bimbo, Bimbo we love Bimbo!
Bimbo, Bimbo, Bimbo es mejor!

Bimbo for the kids,
For Pop and for Mam;
It's the kind of dullest taste
That suits everyone.
No-one knows the
Secret of the Bimbo fame -
Perhaps it's not the bread:
It's the Bimbo name!

Bimbo, Bimbo, Bimbo we love Bimbo!
Bimbo, Bimbo, Bimbo es mejor!

Next time I go looking for a loaf of tasty bread
I'll remember just what the ad man said:
Never choose a bread with a catchy name -
Sounds like something different
But it's Bimbo all the same!

Bimbo, Bimbo, Bimbo we love Bimbo!
Bimbo, Bimbo, Bimbo es mejor!

*Bimbo is the most famous make of sliced bread in Spain

OH NO, MOS-QUI-TO!

Oh no, Mos-qui-to!
Buzzing round your head
You know that sound -
It's the fizzy little creature
Flying all around.
Oh no, Mos-qui-to!
But when's he gonna stop
Where's he gonna land?
May be on my leg,
May be on your hand.
Oh no, Mos-qui-to!
When I turn the light on
You're nowhere to be seen;
May be you're imaginary
May be in a dream.
Oh no, Mos-qui-to!
Back in the dark
You're out again;
I hear you flapping
About me, and then....
Oh no, Mos-qui-to!
I feel you crawl
On the inside of my ear.
I take aim silently
Then THWACK! You disappear.
Oh no, Mos-qui-to!
I'm too tired
To bother any more;
I hope you cannot sleep
As you listen to me snore.

Oh no, oh no, oh no,
Oh no, Mosquito, Mosquito, Mosquito, Mosquito.
I wake up in the morning,
Turn on all the lights;
You've been all night a-partying -
I'm a mass of mozzy bites!